What's Missing?
What's Missing?

ALCOHOLIC, BRAWLER, CHEATER, ADULTERER, DRUG USER, spendthrift, gambler, liar, sex addict, thief, bully, abuser, victim of crime or abuse, hopeless, lost, destitute, suicidal. When you look in the mirror, do you see any of these staring back at you? Have you made foolish choices that may have cost you your marriage, job, or home or even landed you in jail?

When looking back at your life, as if staring at a portrait of your past, does the picture seem empty, stained even? Do you wonder, "What's missing?"

If reflecting on your life fills your heart with despair, it's a sign that you've chosen the wrong road. Getting high, sleeping around, blowing your paycheck on gambling, or buying impulsively to fill an emotional void are the ways of the (fallen) world. They're snares to trap people. Following your base

appetites will only lead you deeper into a hole of depression that you can't crawl out of—not without help.

If you're already at the bottom of a deep pit, don't despair—there is a way out. Someone loves you enough to provide the help you need. That person is Jesus Christ, and He doesn't care what path you've chosen in life. He wants to lead you back to the path to Salvation.

You CAN change who you are and how you feel. It begins by realizing that you've taken a wrong turn. With the right tour guide and the right map, you can find your way. The tour guide is Jesus Christ, and the map is the Bible.

Maybe you feel hopeless and believe it's too late to change. It's never too late. Jesus Christ is not crippled by your past, and he cares greatly about your future. He walked in this fallen world, and He knows how hard it is. If you're ready to crawl out of that hole, Jesus Christ's hand is reaching out for you. You need only take it and believe in your heart that He died for you. He died for all the wrong you've done, to give you a second chance and a new life.

When you give your life to Jesus Christ, your soul—the eternal part of you that lives forever—is saved. Once He has hold of you, He'll never let you go. God works miraculous wonders every day, and He may heal your troubles and your addictions the moment you accept Jesus Christ as your personal savior. Or He may not. But accepting Christ begins the process of transformation. With Jesus Christ in your life, God can give you the strength to rise above past sins that may have left ugly scars and unpleasant consequences. He can even use the consequences of sin to make you into the person He wants you to be. Your life will begin to turn around. Without Christ, the pain, bondage, and hopelessness will continue.

Still, there is nothing wrong with expecting a miracle. Miracles can, do, and will happen once you've given yourself wholeheartedly to Christ. Before we discuss the miraculous power that God has to transform your life, let's take a hard look at ourselves by answering some questions.

> **Note:** These are tough, in-your-face questions. But, if you want to crawl out of that hole of addiction and depression, you should answer them honestly. You don't have to write down the answers. Just search your heart for the truth as you reflect on your past and present.

*Are you in financial peril, in fear of losing your home, or unable to pay your bills?

*Are you stealing to make ends meet or support your addictions?

*Are you having relationship or marital troubles?

*Are you having an affair or cheating on your spouse?

*Are you lying to your friends and family to hide secrets you don't want anyone to know?

*Were you ever abused physically, sexually, or emotionally?

*Are you addicted to sex, spending, gambling, Internet porn, drugs, pills, or alcohol?

*Are you trading sex for favors or money?

*Are you destroying your body by overeating, drugs, or drinking?

*Are you filled with constant anger?

*Are you depressed, grieving, or resentful?

*Do your actions and words reflect a bad or negative person?

If you answered YES to just one question on the list, you're on the wrong path physically, emotionally, and spiritually. You can find a better way to live, a way that allows the old you that created these negative situations to fade away so that a new you can be reborn to experience a life of fulfillment, leading to eternal life in Heaven. This new life can fill that void in your heart; stomp out those urges for sex, drugs, and spending; and give you a new sense of worth and purpose.

Only Jesus Christ can help you turn the answers to these questions from YES to NO. The Lord doesn't want you to live in misery, ill health, or poverty. He wants you to live a life worthy of His approval, which leads to eternal life. He loves you and wants your love in return.

Life doesn't always turn out as we think it should. When we don't get the job we want, when our spouse leaves us, or when we fall in with the wrong crowd, hope can fade, despair can set in, and addiction can result. When life takes a wrong turn, many fail to seek the answers to their downfall. Instead, they accept the consequences and look for ways to bury their pain and fill the void inside. But this void will always exist unless you fill it with Jesus. Trying to fill this void by satisfying our base instincts starts a snowball that grows bigger and bigger until our despair has spun out of control.

At what point did that snowball start rolling? What made you so depressed that you turned to sex, drugs, alcohol, spending, lying, cheating, or stealing to fill that void? You may have believed in a man named Jesus, but it's not the same as a true, personal relationship with Jesus Christ. When we have God, we have the spiritual means to face any downfall in our lives, whether we run into financial troubles, lose a loved one to a tragic death, or are confronted with any other emotionally charged experience. When you are in Christ, the Lord is always there to catch you when you fall. Nothing else can replace the sensation of being filled with the supernatural love of God.

Many will say they've accepted Christ and felt the spirit of God yet have fallen victim to bad circumstances or made terrible choices. That's because humans are sinful by nature. We make choices every day that affect our lives. Our ability to choose our path is a gift from God. It's called free will, and it means the decisions we make can affect us positively or negatively. Making choices is like standing at a fork in the road. When we choose the wrong fork by following our sinful nature, we bring negative consequences upon ourselves. With Christ, you'll know which road to choose. Still, we're not perfect and we may falter. We will occasionally choose the wrong path and may face troubled times. But with Christ, there is no situation we cannot overcome.

When you choose to be faithful to your spouse, it's your choice. Whether you steal or offer your last dollar to someone in need, it's your choice. When you choose to accept or not accept Christ as your personal savior, it's your choice. Choices can put you in the bondage of depression or help you live a happier life by abiding in a higher moral standard, which we learn by studying the life of Christ. When you choose right, and you choose Christ, the things that oppress and depress you begin to fade away.

Some say they have no choice but to take the wrong road because they're a product of their parents and their environment. They've grown up knowing nothing else, which is why they fall short. It's time for some role-playing. Let's put ourselves in someone's shoes to see how easy it is to turn from eternal death to eternal life.

Suppose you grew up in a broken home and began stealing and doing drugs as a teenager. You landed in foster homes, juvenile detention centers, and now jail. Why? Because you were convinced that a thieving drug addict was all you'd ever amount to.

You're not alone. Many people feel trapped, forced to live out their lives as a product of their past. It's a lie! If you feel trapped, with no way out, then it's time to let go and let God!

Imagine that you've been sentenced to life in prison with no parole. Close your eyes and visualize a life behind bars. Scary thought, isn't it?

Now imagine yourself standing before the judge as he prepares to pass sentence. You stare up at the judge with a look of despair and then notice the compassion in his eyes. He doesn't want you to spend the rest of your life in prison. Right before he slams the gavel, he pauses, looks down at you, and says, "I will forgive you of ALL of your past crimes and set you free, if only you can truthfully tell me with all your heart that you are sorry, you ask for my forgiveness, and you promise to follow the law."

Surely you would take the judge's offer. The Lord God Almighty offers you clemency. All you have to do is believe that His son, Jesus Christ, died for you to take away your sins so that you could be born again and live a life worth meaning.

There is no better offer than to accept Jesus Christ into your life. God doesn't make mistakes. YOU were born for a reason, and that reason wasn't for drugs, prostitution, failed marriages, stealing, porn addiction, or living a life of deception.

FYI—If you received this booklet from fellow Christians passing it out on the street, the purpose wasn't to get you into their church, though you'd always be welcome, I'm sure. The purpose is to show you how to have a personal relationship with our Lord Jesus Christ so that you can live a happy, fruitful life, enjoying the glory of the Father. You do need the companionship of other brothers and sisters in Christ that a church can provide, but it begins with Christ. Many use the church as an excuse to turn away from Christianity. They say church isn't for them because it has too many hypocrites. This isn't about church; it's about your relationship with God. Everything around you was made possible because of God. He is the great provider. We wouldn't be alive without God. We wouldn't have love, food, shelter, or happiness without God. Without Him, we have nothing.

Most important, He gave us the greatest gift of all, the gift of His son. What we do with that gift is up to us. When you accept the gift of Jesus Christ, you become a light in the dark. Each person, as they accept Jesus, radiates more light, and the more light in the world, the brighter we grow to help stamp out the darkness. Do you want to live in the light or live in the dark?

What's holding you back? Are you afraid of what others might say? Do you feel that Christians aren't cool? Do you think your blaring music, earrings, or arm-sleeve of tattoos aren't accepted by Christ? Do you believe that Christ doesn't fit in with your lifestyle? If you think you can't enjoy life and worship Christ, think again! There are famous athletes, actors, and musicians around the world who love the Lord. If they can profess their love for God, we have no excuses!

Are you ready to turn your life around? Then it's time for a call to action! It begins by giving your life to Christ. Some say they want to give 100% or nothing at all, and since they cannot give 100%, they just slip away, wondering why they can't break a drug habit, why they're stuck in depression, why their relationships are failing. If you simply take the first step today, by accepting the Lord Jesus Christ as your personal savior, the rest will follow!

It's time to submit your application to your new boss. Don't worry about what's on your résumé. It doesn't matter what you've done in your life, you WILL be accepted. The Lord loves everyone. Regardless of your past sins, all will be forgiven when you come to Him, full of love in your heart, truly asking for forgiveness. It can start now!

HOW TO BE SAVED

It begins by confessing your sins to God. Admit you've sinned against Him, and ask for forgiveness through prayer. Here's a simple prayer that might help you say what you want:

> *"I believe in my heart that Jesus is Lord, that he died for my sins and was raised from the dead, so that I may live an eternal life. I confess my sins to You and ask that you please forgive me. I ask that you take my life and make it Yours. Please fill me with Your Holy Spirit."*

If you said this prayer or something similar, and believed it with all your heart, you can now know you were saved. We know it's true, because God's Word says so, in Romans 10:9-10

If you confess with your mouth that Jesus is Lord and believe in your heart that God raised him from the dead, you will be saved. For it is by believing in your heart that you are made right with God, and it is by confessing with your mouth that you are saved. (Salvation: deliverance from sin and its eternal consequences).

NOW THAT I'M SAVED, WHAT HAPPENS NEXT?

Now that you're saved and have dedicated your life to Christ, the real work begins. Don't expect smooth sailing. We're still human, and our sinful natures still beckon to us daily. It's a battle, but if you're willing to fight that battle, the rewards will be everlasting life, a way out of your afflictions, and a road to a better life. Like any other job, you have to work at it.

To begin changing your ways requires that you study the guidebook of moral living known as the Bible. Pick one up and read every day, starting today. Find a Bible-based church. Don't worry about what you look like, where you come from, or how you dress. Christ looks at what's on the inside, not on the outside. Otherwise, rock stars like Alice Cooper and Brian "Head" Welch would be tossed to the side along with their tattoos, earrings, and heavy metal music. You need like-minded friends and family to help you grow spiritually.

To kick-start the learning experience, read a chapter from the book of Proverbs every day. Proverbs is the book of wise living and will help you become a better person morally and develop a successful attitude. For each day of the month, read a chapter—Chapter One on the first, and Chapter Thirty-One on the 31st. If there aren't thirty-one days in the month, read until you finish the book, then start again with Chapter One on the first day of the next month.

But accepting Christ, reading the Bible, and attending church isn't enough. You must develop a loving relationship with God that encourages you to help others in need by offering aid and spreading the Word of God. This loving relationship will be strengthened once you begin a daily devotion to prayer. Prayer is our communication path to the

Lord. Through prayer we ask for aid for ourselves and can ask that aid be sent to others to protect all God's children in time of need. Prayer lifts our spirits and guides us through good times and bad. Prayer is also a time to ask for forgiveness of our sins and to thank the Lord for all He has done for us.

Even if you're surrounded by people who suffer the same addictions or afflictions as you, you can still find your way out. And you can help them find their way out. The love of Christ and prayer are the keys. We know that prayer will work for you because God tells us to pray and promises to answer our prayers. He is faithful and not a man that He should lie.

We need prayer. When we pray, Christ reaches out His hand to pull us out of the bottom of that hole. The following Bible verses address issues that may need prayer and guidance. Learn and recite the verse that applies to the area of your life most in need.

> **Note:** These verses can be incorporated into daily prayer, which should become a staple in your life. Pray for forgiveness, for blessing, for others that need your support, and thank the Lord for your abundance. Pray upon waking, bless every meal, pray upon retiring to bed, pray whenever you feel the urge. Everything comes from God, and prayer brings you closer to Him.

SALVATION
If you confess with your mouth Jesus as Lord, and believe in your heart that God raised Him from the dead, you will be saved.

Romans10:9.

ADDICTION
No temptation has overtaken you except what is common to mankind. And God is faithful; he will not let you be tempted beyond what you can bear. But when you are tempted, he will also provide a way out so that you can endure it. 1 Corinthians 10:13
Verses to look up concerning addiction:

Hebrews 2:18, 1 Peter 5:8-9

ANGER

In your anger do not sin. Do not let the sun go down while you are still angry. Ephesians 4:26

Verses to look up concerning anger:

Matthew 6:14, Proverbs 14:29

CONFIDENCE

I can do all this through him who gives me strength. Philippians 4:13

Verses to look up concerning lack of confidence:

Isaiah 43:2, 1 John 5:14-15

DEPRESSION

The righteous cry out, and the LORD hears them; he delivers them from all their troubles. Psalm 34:17

Verses to look up concerning depression:

Psalm 147:3, Matt 11:28-30

FINANCIAL TROUBLE

And my God will supply every need of yours according to his riches in glory in Christ Jesus. Philippians 4:19

Verses to look up concerning financial trouble:

Psalm 23:1, Matthew 6:33

FORGIVENESS OF YOUR SINS

If we confess our sins, he is faithful and just and will forgive us our sins and purify us from all unrighteousness. 1 John 1:9

Verses to look up concerning forgiveness of your sins:

Psalm 103:12, 2 Corinthians 5:17

FORGIVENESS TO OTHERS

And when you stand praying, if you hold anything against anyone, forgive them, so that your Father in heaven may forgive you your sins. Mark 11:25

Verses to look up concerning the forgiveness of others:

Ephesians 4:31-32, Matthew 6:14

GRIEF
For his anger lasts only a moment, but his favor lasts a lifetime; weeping may stay for the night, but rejoicing comes in the morning. Psalm 30:5
Verses to look up concerning grief:

Psalm 147:3, 1 Peter 5:7

ILLNESS (PHYSICAL AND MENTAL)
Is anyone among you sick? Let them call the elders of the church to pray over them and anoint them with oil in the name of the Lord. 15 And the prayer offered in faith will make the sick person well; the Lord will raise them up. If they have sinned, they will be forgiven. 16 Therefore confess your sins to each other and pray for each other so that you may be healed. The prayer of a righteous person is powerful and effective. James 5:14-16
Verses to look up concerning physical and mental illness:

Jeremiah 30:17, Psalm 103:3

LONELINESS
Turn to me and be gracious to me, for I am lonely and afflicted. Psalm 25:16
Verses to look up concerning loneliness:

Psalm 68:6

MARITAL TROUBLES
Wives, submit yourselves to your husbands, as is fitting in the Lord. Husbands, love your wives and do not be harsh with them. Colossians 3:18-19
Verses to look up concerning martial troubles:

Ephesians 5:28, Hebrews 13:4

MONEY/PROSPERITY/SUCCESS
Keep this Book of the Law always on your lips; meditate on it day and night, so that you may be careful to do everything written in it. Then you will be prosperous and successful. Joshua 1:8
Verses to look up concerning money/prosperity/success:

Deuteronomy 8:18, Proverbs 6:13

SEXUAL IMMORALITY

Flee from sexual immorality. All other sins a person commits are outside the body, but whoever sins sexually, sins against their own body. 19 Do you not know that your bodies are temples of the Holy Spirit, who is in you, whom you have received from God? You are not your own; 20 you were bought at a price. Therefore honor God with your bodies. 1 Corinthians 6:18-20

Verses to look up concerning sexual immorality:

1 John 2:16-17, Matthew 5:27-29

WORRY AND FEAR

So do not fear, for I am with you; do not be dismayed, for I am your God. I will strengthen you and help you; I will uphold you with my righteous right hand. Isaiah 41:10

Verses to look up concerning worry and fear:

Psalm 23:4-5, Matthew 6:31-34

DON'T stop here! These are but a few of thousands of verses. There's much wisdom to be learned from the Bible that will apply to all aspects of your life. If you don't have a Bible, find one that suits you. It doesn't matter if it's a King James, New King James, New International Version, New Living Testament, or any translation that helps you better understand the Word. Read the Bible every day and add verses to the end of this booklet; verses that speak to you. Think of the Bible as soul food; as a big steak feeds your belly, the Bible feeds your soul.

Accept Christ, read and apply the Word, add prayer to your daily life, and watch your life change forever. The truth is, you're going to live forever, be it in paradise or in torment. If you haven't given your life to Christ yet, know that He loves you and He is patiently waiting for you. Life will be Hell without him.

Therefore, if anyone is in Christ, he is a new creation, the old has gone, the new has come.
2 Corinthians 5:17

Verses for Eternal Salvation

Book	Chap/verse	Scripture Language

Verses for Conquering Addiction

Book	Chap/verse	Scripture Language

Verses for Calming Anger

Book	Chap/verse	Scripture Language

Verses to Instill Confidence

Book	Chap/verse	Scripture Language

Verses for Easing Depression

Book	Chap/verse	Scripture Language

Verses for Overcoming Financial Trouble

Book	Chap/verse	Scripture Language

Verses That Show the Way to Forgiveness of Your Sins

Book	Chap/verse	Scripture Language

Verses Promoting the Forgiveness of Others

Book	Chap/verse	Scripture Language

Verses for Handling Grief

Book	Chap/verse	Scripture Language

Verses for Battling Mental and Physical Illness

Book	Chap/verse	Scripture Language

Verses for Dealing With Loneliness

Book	Chap/verse	Scripture Language

Verses for Resolving Marital Troubles

Book	Chap/verse	Scripture Language

Verses Concerning Money/Prosperity/Success

Book	Chap/verse	Scripture Language

Verses for Defeating Sexual Immorality

Book	Chap/verse	Scripture Language

Verses for Dissolving Worry and Fear

Book	Chap/verse	Scripture Language

VENDERA PUBLISHING

Interior Design by Daniel Middleton | www.scribefreelance.com
Cover Design by Molly Burnside | www.crosssidedesigns.com

ISBN: 978-1-936307-23-4
Published in the United States of America

To obtain printed copies of *What's Missing* at print cost, please contact Jaime Vendera through admin@venderapublishing.com